# A Saving Bannister

Poems
by
Wendy Woodward

Publication © Modjaji Books 2015

First published by Modjaji Books Pty Ltd

PO Box 121 Rondebosch, 7701, South Africa

modjaji.books@gmail.com

**www.modjajibooks.co.za**

ISBN 978-1-920590-80-2

**Edited by** Fiona Zerbst

**Design and layout by** Louise Topping (Topping Design)

Front cover image: Shutterstock.com

Poetry—
but what sort of thing is poetry?
Many a shaky answer
has been given to this question.
But I do not know and do not know and hold
on to it,
as to a saving bannister.

Wisława Szymborska

# Contents

# Poetry

*"I ..hold on to it as to a saving bannister"*

Across the abyss a bannister goes,
a railing on a ledge
over sullen darkness,
leading its intermediaries
to stairs up and down,
rooms that begin and do not end,
halls of light (but rarely glory),
alcoves peopled by rain spiders and slow breathing.

Sometimes, with our hands on the bannister,
we stumble to windows,
to vistas of plains and steppes
with Mazeppa always in the distance,
bound to a wild mare who will stop
only when her heart does.

Seas, too, swim to windows,
now the ice has melted,
replete with endlessly questing bears – ,
for what bannister can save them now?

# Dodging the Monastic Gaze

A new road through landslide scree
brought us to these pillars
tilting after the earthquake,
ornate designs flaking
at ------ monastery in high Sikkim.

An adolescent monk
serves cups and cups of tea,
before our audience
with the Rinpoche,
whose gaze drills light
into ignorant minds.

In the shrine room
the Buddha keeps calm,
his head at his draped feet,
but we are silenced
by his loss. Next door,
Mahakala roars triumphant,
trampling our egos
from a blue horse
with an all-seeing eye
on his shapely, blue rump.

Up the hill,
near the Retreat Centre,
tantric demonesses
on all fours
mimic bodily desires.
Their breasts loll, their faces leer.

Passing them, we circle the building,
quietly,
in sacred space.

The monks
spend three cloistered years here
with teachings and practices;
yet even they have needs
we find, as we dodge slops
coursing from the parapet.

But our female urgencies are taboo,
the monks must not see us,
no tourist toilets
exist and the nearby woods are sparse
and too close. At the end of the first
circle walked, we encounter a lean-to
shed slanting down the slope to the monastery.

We hope that Mahakala's eyes
are closed for once,
the demonesses otherwise occupied.
We even ignore our pacing drivers close by,
and pray that the local gods will understand
as we pee into the Himalayan wind,
utterly liberated.

# Punch and Judy

What *did* they think
they were teaching us,
our mothers (fathers always elsewhere)
when they sat us down,
primped and starched
in our flared party dresses
and mohair boleros
in front of the anachronism
of a Punch and Judy show?

The acting out
of Punch's roaring violence,
the spectacle of his rage,
set me weeping
into the bolero's fluff.

But Judy, irrepressible,
has stayed with me
through the years,
a trope for endurance—
always bobbing up after tragedy
and trauma. Her resilience
has shredded my knees on the theatre floor
for too long, though.

It's the dog
who inspires me now,
with his agency and cunning;
and for his insistence
on the rights of small, brown dogs
to fair play,
on a starved, truncheoned stage.

# Founders' Day, Girls High School, Eastern Cape

Here I am in the marquee to house all the girls
*Let us Now Praise Famous Men*
and us—very Old Girls
*And Our Fathers That Begat Us*
as the sonorous intoning begins
*Such As Did Bear Rule in their Kingdoms*
with the choir girls harmonising
*Men Renowned For Their Power*
just as they did forty years before.

I sit, stunned at the verbiage.
*Leaders of the People*
At tea, in the indifferent school hall
*By Their Counsel and By Their Knowledge*
I mention my 'concern' to the principal,
but he deflects me, deftly, like a slow hockey ball,
over cream scones and cupcakes.
*Such as Found out Musical Tunes and Recited Verses in Writing*
"It wouldn't rhyme," he is adamant, "to put in women."

He is right, of course; more right than he knows.
It wouldn't rhyme with the whole of Deuteronomy
or the Bible,
or the ancient Old Boys' network
which still informs this girls' school
on another foundered day.

# Icarus revisited

Wollongong Beach, NSW, Australia

The boy-child moves slowly,
swollen in clothes and clumsiness,
his wings clipped, too close to the bone.
The woman pouts with mother-love
grounding him with accessories,
and bags of fried Asian delicacies.

The man bristles, pounding the air,
the football useless under his arm.
Struts for wings remain in his knapsack,
wax and feathers are taken by the wind;
the boy's trucks ascend and descend/
ascend and descend the ramp of sand.

From the distant beach to the promontory
where we stand, a swimmer dodges
the Scylla and Charybdis of rocks far below.
The boy keens: Stop! Go
back! Stop! Go back! His mother bends
to his grief. His father dribbles the ball away.

The man below glides on in an empty sea,
heedlessly, joyfully towards the  horizon.

# Playing with the Leviathan

*In the last three hours of the day, God sits and plays with the Leviathan, as is written: "you made the Leviathan in order to play with it"* (Talmud Avodah Zarah)

He is as long as a small town,
as broad as a high street peopled
with shops and flags,
yet here he is in the bay,
hefting himself cautiously
out of the waters onto a dryness
that makes his skin itch.

I am not God (or even a minor dakini)
but I invite him to play—
to put one fin into a saraband
that rattles the rooks' nests
in the bell tower.

It is a stately dance
with much courtesy—
only when he returns to the ocean
do we romp
and dive
and lobtail
until the moon glistens on his flanks,
beside the fins I have grown.

# Walking through walls

## For Beryl

Stopped by particles of doubt
I remain here transfixed
(moths under pins come to mind).
How to extricate oneself?

My inner debate eases
the squeeze a little, but
not till the certainty settles
of the porousness of all things,
does the brick shift,
the concrete loosen,
    infinitesimally.

Only then can I spring
through to the other side—
    a little dirty,
    a little stiff,
but ready to walk
through another wall,
    soon,
    soon.

# The Pineapple Market

For Adrian Mitchell

It was my family's refrain—
"the bottom's fallen out
of the pineapple market."

I saw those heavy baskets
on the workers' heads,
pineapples cascading around them
through the severed cane
as fruit rotted in the sun
and baboons scarpered
with pines prickling their armpits.

It was my father's refrain after his 'nervous breakdown'
(when the machinery jolted to a stop)
as he breathed into a paper bag
fishing and fishing (as the doctors ordered),
pulling leerfish from the sea.

On holiday at Wave Crest,
not far enough from the bankrupt farm,
I schemed, in waking and in sleep,
how to run from the tidal wave
about to fill the horizon with white spume,
curling, as it roared towards us,
        insistently,
smelling, always, of pineapples.

# "Breaking glass behind a closed door"

In memory of GM, my late father's oldest friend,
ninety-five years old at the time of this visit

Trying to remember the past
is like breaking glass
behind a closed door.

You cannot reach it,
though your hand goes through the door
to what is splintering in
a room beyond,
memories mere images
of light slanting in late afternoons.

Here he is now,
in a room cavernous
with silence.
The son who died drops in each day.
The son who farms nearby never comes—
or so he tells me—
though he himself visits the farm
without leaving the room.

He remembers my father but I—
who loved his horses for years,
riding them to beaches and in shows—
am a blank.

He tells his own stories,
existing in a mind
slowly mouldering away

like green wainscoting
on a house seen dimly
through dark cedars.

But who is to say
that the long-dead son
does not saunter down
the scrubbed corridors
repeating the old jokes
of scratching his pigs
caringly, between their ample shoulders
en route to  slaughter?

Even I can hear his laughter now
as I fade,
with my ghost-smiles and chatter,
into oblivion
behind the closing door.

# A Midrash for Lot's Wife

For Dorian

Lot's hospitality for the angels
fell within his blustering revenge
against all I had loved.

Even so, I baked them bread,
though the oven had lost its flame,
drew water to wash their white feet
though the wells were far from our walls,
beyond the theatres and circuses—
places of lightness and laughter,
Lot feared and hated.

No wonder our wedded daughters
spurned his visions of Sodom's demise.
Their husbands scoffed at his jaw set against them,
their children at marbles ignored his rants.

How could I leave them all –
and the places that knew me –
where the white goats blazed in yellow wheat
and vines trailed purple nectar
as bullocks nudged my cart
along the tracks bright with gazanias?

When the mob came to our home
desiring the angels,
he pimped our young daughters instead.
Once away from the city, I knew he would take them to wife,
leaving me with my mouth stopped in a cave.

What use would I be then?
Better to stay.
Better by far to be a pillar –
as impermanent as all I had loved –
of salt, beloved by goats and bullocks,
and the little klipspringer
who comes stepping softly to me now,
immune to the apocalypse behind her,
to the dull fire and hurtling brimstone
at her pointed, perfect hooves.

# Bird Calls

For Jaclyn, on a bird walk in Mtunzini, Zululand

She worries about recorded bird song:
if played indiscriminately back
its messages can only confuse.

What if the news is bad?
Your house is on fire,
your babies are lost,
your mate has migrated
with another of softer feather.

Or too good?
A new mate awaits you,
offering a nest
shining with downy promises.

Believe rather
that nerina trogons
are more astute.
Mozarts all,
they hear the artifice
and come tongue-in-beak to visit us –
only if it pleases them –
in this humid dawn.

or they might turn their faces,
without  distraction,
to the beauties of bark with its fungal moons,
thinking airily of lunch or tea.

# Stories

We will all die from a lack of stories.
Ishi, the last 'wild Indian'
in California in the 1930s,
cossetted by anthropologists,
died of a cold,
but the silence already had him by the throat,
as surely as snaring wire.

The last oyster-catcher
on the larval rocks
pit-pits conversations
for feathered ghosts
rehearsing the minutiae of her day:
the squabbling seagull,
the morsel lost to the sea.

The last Knysna elephant
lives with such loss, too.
She speaks to whales
who hear her sonar rumble.
They pass with speed
seldom now
that their world is deafened.
They tell of lost precision,
of depth soundings
adrift in darkening seas.

The silence subsides,
a little, for the old elephant,
at such encounters.

Her stories creak into mobility,
but the comfort never accompanies her
as she returns, solitary once again,
to blend with the boulders,
solid like beloved companions,
yet irrevocably speechless.

# Facing a Dog (Cecilia Forest)

Contra Levinas

He often disappears,
chasing narratives
of small presences into the forest.
Today he is absent too long
till I hear him barking up the high kloof
as if from another life
    or legend
and then down he careens
back legs over-tracking forelegs
along the rocky incline.

At first, I think he is carrying a twig,
but as he gets closer
the porcupine quill cannot be denied.
It enters at one nostril
and comes out the other side—
a ritual piercing of a beloved face.

I am pleased, momentarily, that porcupines
still live in the crevices we have left them.
Then I return to his pain and disfigurement,
so stoically accepted.

As we walk down the mountain
he holds his head strategically.
I want to babble to each dog-walker,
but they greet only the human-us,
not the animal in the company.

Once he is quietly home and ministered to,
I wonder at such lacunae,
at the disregard of the animal face—
the foregoing of a greeting,
the indifference to a forest full of stories.

# Roundstone Vineyards, near Riebeek Kasteel

A quietness here
I could almost be persuaded by,
in the felt silence of the Kasteelberg
and the clouded Paardeberg.

But nature is not itself, nor is it romantic.
Beyond the hills are chicken batteries,
where a notice tells us
*Drive Safe, Eat Safe!*
as a comic-book rooster
waves happily from
a car that he steers,
even as he dwarfs it in size.

A tractor fusses with its trench-making
behind the cottage,
where a bokmakierie slams himself
into a glass chimera
so intrepidly and foolishly
that he bloodies his beak.

The vineyards below
have been sprayed with poisons
and there are feuds on these farms:
some workers abscond,
preferring roadworks to vines.

Cloud shadows
patchwork the fields of wheat
across the valley--
a rural picturesque
that seeks to beguile,
without ever cohering
the fractured afternoon.

# Jazz Lament

Before me
the pianist in black and white
plays the truth
of other incarnations--
of a man who imagined the dance,
with the lover he never found—
her skirt swishing the door
as she left for altogether elsewhere.

I wish he had found her somewhere,
in the haze of a saxophone,
in the desire of a melody,
but he missed her once
and was never allowed to try again.

They are dead now, my parents,
gone through the Bardos
to Buddha-knows-where.

I remain in the ballroom,
empty of chords and caresses,
bereft of the dance they never had.

# Clove Ghost

Discreetly, through flickering poplars
and over spruce, clipped lawn,
the ghost came to us
on our first night together.
She came from Java, perhaps,
on her own spice route,
centuries ago,
to slavery in the Cape.

We can only guess
at the mystery
of her presence
which we can smell—
the aura of cloves,
the miasma of ginger,
in the green Newlands night.

Was she summoned
by our luminosity
to a memory of love,
a slight sliver of happiness
where sickly vines once
held back the wilderness?

Or was it pain
which drew her to us,
as she mourned,
her lack
of what we had begun?

# The Ear of the Donkey

For Liesl

Going into the ear of the donkey
I sing into her mind
which chants back,
mesmerising me
with the rapture of the herd.

In response I grow donkey hide,
long legs, shapely, for the dance of us all,
and ears sensitive to our communal music.

I breathe into our lungs,
practise arpeggios in our throats
and step into our syncopated rhythm.
Together we swim into night air
way above the foothill-village.

We forage beyond the men's fire
but we keep our shadow selves close,
immobilised at intervals
by the demon calls of the jackals
and other hungry ghosts.

At dawn we nuzzle
the little god
of the path among
benevolent rocks
and nurturing deodars.

Even as he asserts himself
a trifle loudly, with his small
red-burnished trident,
his beard curling to his dhoti,
he accepts our blessing
as we trot past,
humming the herd together
on our journey ever upwards.

# Mistaking pigeon poo for the sound of the universe

*Arno Penzias and Robert Woodrow Wilson won the Nobel Prize in 1978 for recording cosmic microwave background radiation which, they surmised, was the sound left over from the rather loud Big Bang signalling the start of the universe*

First they blamed the hiss
of their great ear,
recording the sound
of the universe,
on the pigeon poo
whitening the surface
of the Holmdel Horn Antenna

The pigeons were deported,
humanely elsewhere,
but they flew home (as homing pigeons do)
skilfully,
 without maps or mnemonics.

The scientists sought sharp shooters,
to dispatch the pigeons,
less kindly now,
to elsewhere in the universe
(heaven knows where pigeon souls alight)

But the hiss continued hissing,
proving it was the sound of the universe,
the soft sibilants of the Big Bang
years later,

not the layer of pigeon poo
dropped by birds
drawn to the soft soughing
    of the spheres,
as it interlaced,
consummately,
with their loving trills.

# The Uncle Poems

## Sharks

The little sand shark
had no intention of shifting elements,
but there it was, anyway,
entirely dead
on the sands of my childhood.

My uncle's sleight of hand
returned it to the breakers
then captured it bare-handed in the surf
(playing brave fisherman,
while we laughed)

My young cousin
saw only the heroism
of his father, not the trickery,
and took the fish (named Casper,
after the cartoon friendly ghost)
all the way to Mthatha,
where the corpse decayed
on top of the aviary,
until one night it appeared,
lovingly laid on the pillow
next to his sleeping form.

Now, as adults, the story re-surfaces
when we meet in the Antipodes,
and we amuse a new friend or a new wife,
 who has joined the ranks of the shark-catcher.

Casper brings a lightness
as the tale glances off memories
of the love of a boy for a dead shark
and the belief in his talisman;
before we knew of the shark fins
of a black and white Dodge
that killed his father, not many years later,
before we knew what his father had survived
to tease the boy in the waves—
the POW camp where he practiced dentistry
on the Japanese guards
for another mouthful of rice.

We skim these horrors
silently, like stones across salt water.
Far easier to place a stinking shark
next to a smiling, sleeping boy.

## Turnings

You never hear about alternatives that did not work:
"I took the wrong turning and I died"
spoken by a spirit from the Other Side.

We did not think of that
at Sunday tea , when Uncle Gerald
would tell us of taking
the *right* turning out of the sinking
torpedoed Hermes
("My mate told me to go with him—
I never saw him again").
After hours in the oiled water,
rescue, then up the gangway
of the hospital ship
to the open-armed welcome of the nurse
who handed out cigarettes (dispensing death after all),
launching him into a habit
that would take years to renounce.

Gerald told his tale, always, with humour
and irony—
or was it astonishment
at his luck
that he had crossed
to our suburban lounge (its delicate
figurines dustless in a display cabinet)
to eat coconut tart with cream,
as he served up his sanitised tale,
again and again?

# The Horse and the Crocodile

Stretching alongside the horse and the crocodile
on the couch of our doctor
I can't help but edge closer to the palomino,
plaiting his copious mane just as the *nagmerrie* birds do,
(although I lack their twigs and fine beaks).

Simple patterns have to suffice
in the mane that spreads over the couch,
blanketing our two bodies
as I inhale his warmth
to contradict the green tiles of the crocodile.

She shivers a little from the cold
ignoring the birds cleaning her teeth,
to ask a favour—
contact with the woman and the horse,
given the lack of sun
or any electrical artifice that might have
begun in my higher mammalian brain.

The horse and I gaze questions at each other,
then decide on compassion—
idiotic though it may be —
for the cold beast.
We invite her in to the snug plaiting,
the blood beating in our veins.

There we lie, a little stiffly at first—
but gradually horse and I breathe together
and dream
of the night we warmed the crocodile
with our bodies and brains
on the buttoned-down couch
of our doctor.

# The Minotaur comes to our picnic

Give me a glow-worm, not Ariadne and her silly string,
a being of tunnels who is his own light.
He will guide me to the Minotaur
simmering at the end of the labyrinth.
Settling on the ceiling, he'll offer a silhouette
in this subterranean cave of the one who slowly murders
the heroes who trundle up the path to his lair.

How the beast smiles at their jingling footsteps,
swords reflecting the gleams of their little lights,
soon to be snuffed out.

Coming into the day could be deadly
for this heavy hybrid,
for he lacks experience of openness,
yet he commits to it, trotting fatly down bone-littered corridors.
Knights in armour flatten themselves as we pass,
but I have him by the nose as he steams,
sulphurously, towards the sunlight.

Once on the surface, we fear him less,
decorate the curls on his forehead with lilacs.
He plays a little, in the fynbos, delighting in our company
but tires, soon, of the exercise, his eyes wincing at the light.

When he snores, we consider piercing his hapless heart,
but we need him below, fulminating in the darkness,
testing the bravery of our smug suitors.

We feed him pine nuts and cherries
when he wakes and show him the entrance of his tunnel

which he staggers into, tripping drowsily
on glistening hooves.

He smiles at the edge of the darkness,
promising return, with a tally of his conquests
chalked mnemonically, for our benefit,
on granite walls.

# Masquerade

She left her house for the last time,
on a summer's day,
her life packed into bags and boxes
by the sister she had always loved
betraying her now into suitcases
that ended up in a place called 'home'
    (it was never that)
and 'nursing'
    (but not that, either),
the place, in its heyday a hotel.

No wonder she was confused:
a hotel guest nurtured a doll;
another crooned and rocked
what self she had left.
My reasonable mother lodged
in Bedlam for safety
where inmates called for liberation,
nurses timed shifts without end,
a place of dementia and burnt cabbage.

Only seagulls told of other places.
The sparrows didn't:
   having sold out for crumbs,
    they were part of the grime and greyness.

When we visited, we
composed our faces anew in the passage,
we neglected to mention her body,
turning like an old sunflower towards the earth,
or the gyre of her illness
that whirled her into stasis and a bed with clanking sides.

After the hour or so with her
on the gritty verandah,
we chirruped on with our lives,
setting our masks aside on the downward stairs.

But she lived the masquerade,
shielding us, as she always had,
from the long, dying summer.

# My Kudu

lived behind long fences
in the East London Zoo.
Every Sunday morning
I cajoled him with dry bread
from the top of the camp
to the slope where I stood, below him.

My name for him was generic
but I loved his particularity,
his recognition of my call.
His horns, perseverating against the fence,
rasped away the dull sentimentality of Sunday school
with its simpering angels.

I accepted him for what he seemed to be—
prancing down to me for bread.
I did not think to break my heart
over the dispossession
of all that could have kept him wild,
merely offering him crusts,
and the uselessness of a small girl's love.

# Talking to Jasper, in the garden

24 October 2012

This body,
lying in our dug grave,
draped in a deep-blue sheet
lightened with spring flowers,
recalls other bodies—
the brother with leukaemia,
wanting to die;
the mother whose body
I never saw;
the father who was all body,
mind already elsewhere.

But the dog is also himself,
four paws tucked under him,
like a dog leaping on a frieze,
the golden head still beautiful
in its stillness,
his gaze slowly receding
from the earth.

Just an hour before, he twitched
at a spider on his flanks.
Now small gnats settle
on his face with impunity,
as other creatures will,
soon enough.

We can only hope for the quietness
of his ending under the *plectranthus*,
near the pond with its resident Buddha,
with the prayer flags in the syringa above
blessing our animal spirits
as they flutter away.

10 December 2012

I move the hose over your grave,
passing over the sandy soil
to the edges where grass begins
to grow again.
It is barely six weeks
but the garden is reclaiming you,
covering you over with greenness
in an unremarkable way.

Better by far to have planted a tree
whose roots would have reached the bones
of your body, skeletally pruned,
curling tendrils round your ribs,
shifting, imperceptibly, your immobilised tail.
I understand, now, those bereaved
who tend their departed's remains on feast days.
We could unearth your bones
and touch anew the outlines
of a beloved face;
place your skull on the mantelpiece
and thumb noses at impermanence.

19 January 2013
The garden is calmer
now that you lie beneath it.
Your daily inspection
of avocado trees,
compost heap,
drains and driveway
do not distract
the courting doves
or the prising hadedas
from their intentions.

Plates on the ground are safe
and food dropped from the table
is untouched.
Yet you have not left irrevocably.
I glimpse your golden tail
sashaying round a corner,
just a little beyond touch
and loving conversation.

# Talking to Mishka, in the garden

30 September 2013

You, who prepared the room for me,
did not prepare us for your sudden absence,
or how we'd get your stiff, dear body
into a grave full of roots and pebbles.
We managed finally and you are deep enough,
in your ceremonial Rajasthan shawl
which warmed you throughout winter.

Today, spring attempts solace.
Lemons glow in your honour
as you seem to promenade
high-steppingly between the doves,
laughing and mourning
at the little graveyard
with new jasmine and clivia.

# South African War Horses

In the South African War
326,073 horses died, 51,399 mules—
and that was on the British side.

They died before they got here
from India, Argentina, Australia.
They died
  in ships,
  at the quayside,
  of disease,
  of neglect,
  on the battlefield.

They elude my imaginings,
these half-million beings.

But before me, an image of revenants
from that war: Privates Makin
and Dean pose on their horses in
the bright Molteno sunshine.
Makin's face is shadowed,
a metaphor, perhaps, for what is to come.
Dean's jaw tenses away from our gaze.
They have rifles in their right hands,
cartridge belts bisect their chests.
They lack bravado, these young men;
they do not scoff at their fates.
Their horses are vulnerable, too:
they half-close their eyes to the glare,
their stories already written on their bodies.

Makin's bay lacks muscle
and his tail is docked like that of a *kripvreter*,
cossetted in a stable.
Dean's dappled grey will stand out in rifle sights
from dawn to dusk
and in moonless dark, too.

In this image they remain alive.
The bay muses on the present moment.
The grey flicks her ears to the rider.
Their bodies warm in the midday sun,
their stories, shadowed, directly beneath them
in the quiet, prescient sand.

The Boer horses had already set
their hooves down, below *krantzes*,
over khaki stones
and through *spruits*.
Statistics do not tell
how many of them
collapsed from starvation or exhaustion,
their farms burnt in the veld.

Their names enliven their markings,
their belligerence, their beauty:
Viljoen's *Blesman*, Reitz's *Malpert*, Visser's *Voorslag*,
de Wet's *Fleur*, de la Rey's *Starlight*, Malan's *Very Nice*.

Yet names were no charms
against death,
which came for them soon enough.
Sixty ponies of the Groot Reent Kerels
died in an ice storm, leaving the men
grieving  with saddles in a night
branded forever
by their loss in the killing rain.

Each autumn, old battlefields
come alive with the colour of cosmos,
flowers from the droppings
of horses who ate seed
from Mexico, and beyond
more than a hundred years ago –
little pennants in a remembering wind.

# Avatars of the sublime

Deep suburbia is transformed
from the mundane—
a power cut,
washing half done,
an essay sucked from the screen—
to the otherworldly.

Two fish eagles
straying from Tokai
call to each other
high above
the quotidian—
but not too high
for  glimpses of white feathers
on necks and chests
through red and yellow hibiscus.

# A Cupboard in the Amatholas

A cupboard has floated
on the Cathcart Road
(Hogs at your back)
for many years.

It's an oak cupboard, modest in size,
put there decades ago in response
to two brothers
(our boyfriends at the time).

The younger one told us schoolgirls
that we did not exist
(in the powder-blue Chevrolet
on the Cathcart Road).
The older one
(with intimations, perhaps, of his death
on the hockey field soon after)
was angered by this sophistry.

The younger brother was certain
(on the Cathcart Road)
that cupboards, like us,
lacked solidity,
but I saw it, hovering above
the yellow sublime of the kloofs.
And there it remains—
a constant symbol of non-existence
for all to see.

# The Kiwi Exhibit

Near Rotorua, New Zealand

The little, shuffling kiwi
Is exhibited through a glass darkly.
Her night is our day --
   a small puffball
   safe from possums and cats
but not from a life constantly surveyed.

She feels the spectators' gaze –
I am sure of it –
traversing the same path
that never changes
   its smells in spring,
   its insects at dusk.

Some instinct stirs
in her glass cage.
   She longs for real day
   and real night
without our scrutiny
   and the certain fixities
   at her feathered feet.

# Hidden by the baby grand

Hidden by the baby grand,
she skulks in her lounge,
flicks the switches,
cries on the floor
for the husband who died.

Hidden by the baby grand
and the children of her sons,
she lives quietly
in her house, behind curtains of net,
doors wedged closed against the sun.

Hidden by the baby grand,
her face is silent
to those who love her.
She weeps at night,
smiles quietly in the day.

Only when she sells the piano,
brought from Holland
a century before
on a slow, slow boat,
do we see the grief
scouring her face,
the keys whirling her down
into depths of ebony.

# The Small Rain

Westron wynde, when wylle thou blow,
   The small rayne down can rayne?
Cryst, yf my love were in my armys
   And I in my bed agayne!
(anonymous 15th-century lyric)

You could rule a line
with the confident rain
on Noordhoek Beach,
falling, battleship grey,
large rain that comes with menace,
dull in its lack of poetry,
over the horizon-sea.

Give me the small rain
of the anonymous poet
who speaks of longing for
her beloved, their union
endlessly deferred
by the prevailing wind,
blowing gently over
the years
into my modern,
empathetic heart.

# Samsara

Szymborska loved her dustbin,
diligent poet that she was,
dispatching detritus by the hour.

But I carry more freight—
books that spin me back to childhood newness,
my mother's Egyptian amber,
and any number of clothes to face the world in.

I love, too, the little brass Buddha,
along with the photos on my shrine
of Tashi Jong and the Bodhi tree growing
from the stupa; of the ironic
togden down from his cave.

On the wall, Aunt Olga swanks
side-saddle on her show pony;
my mother simpers in her nursery bonnet.

Only death
will give me a crash-course in giving them up—
the turquoise shard from Samarkand,
the pottery chip from the Flinders Range,
the pregnant stone from Chesil Beach,
all will tilt into landfill.

My books will moulder in charity shops
along with the fictions of my life,
never to be dug up anew
and placed lovingly on shelves or shrines.

*That* will teach me.

# Notes

"Some like Poetry" in *Miracle Fair: Selected Poems of Wisława Szymborska*, translated by Joanna Trzeciak (WW Norton, 2002): 139.

"Breaking Glass behind a closed door" : in my creative writing classes at UWC we play a game, opening a poetry book at random. Whatever phrase the eye falls on provides the impetus for one's own poem. The title of this poem is such a phrase, but unfortunately, I did not keep a note of its origins.

A Midrash for Lot's Wife: Dorian Haarhoff taught me the meaning of 'midrash'. After I had written this poem, I discovered that he had also written about Lot's wife, as had Szymborska.

Facing a Dog (Cecilia Forest): the twentieth century philosopher Emanuel Levinas suggested that if we thought of the 'other' as having a face, we would heed the commandment "Thou shalt not kill." He vacillated, however, about whether an animal can be said to have a face, in this ethical sense.

The Ear of the Donkey: at the first McGregor Poetry Festival Liesl Jobson presented a workshop which drew its title from Robert Bly's collection *Talking into the Ear of the Donkey.* My poem began its life during this workshop.

The Horse and the Crocodile: "Man [sic] finds himself in the predicament that nature has endowed him essentially with three brains which, despite great differences in structure, must function together and communicate with one another. The oldest of these brains is basically reptilian. The second has been inherited from the lower [sic] mammals, and the third is a late mammalian development, which ... has made man peculiarly man. Speaking allegorically of these brains within a brain, we might imagine that when the psychiatrist bids the patient to lie on the couch, he is asking him to stretch alongside a horse and a crocodile." Paul D Maclean, *Journal of Nervous and Mental Disease* (Vol CXXXV, no 4, October 1962). Quoted as an epigraph to Julian Barnes' novel, *Before She Met Me* (1983).

**South African War Horses**: Patricia Schonstein commissioned this poem for her anthology *Africa Ablaze! Poems and Prose Pieces of War and Civil Conflict* (Cape Town: African Sun Press, 2013) in which a slightly different version is published. All historical information is gleaned from Sandra Swart's *Riding High: Horses, Humans and History in South Africa* (Wits University Press 2010). The photograph appears in Johannes Meintjes' Portrait of a South African Village by A. Lomax, Molteno 1894-1909. (Bamboesberg Uitgewers, Molteno 1964).

**Talking to Jasper, in the garden**: an earlier version appeared in the online *Australian Animal Studies Journal*

**A Cupboard in the Amatholas**: the Cathcart Road at this vantage point is close to the Hogsback mountains.

**Hidden by the Baby Grand**: The title is a line from "Women" in *Open Season* by Sally-Ann Murray (Durban : Hard Pressed, 2006, p 55)

**Samsara**: Wisława Szymborska claimed her dustbin as her favourite item of furniture as she dispatched so many rejected poems into it.

Printed in the United States
By Bookmasters